Pebble Plus

How's the Weather?

Today Is Hot

by Martha E. H. Rustad
Consulting Editor: Gail Saunders-Smith, PhD

Consultant: J. Kevin Lavin, executive director
National Weather Association, Charlottesville, Virginia

Capstone press
Mankato, Minnesota

Pebble Plus is published by Capstone Press,
151 Good Counsel Drive, P.O. Box 669, Mankato, Minnesota 56002.
www.capstonepress.com

Printed in the United States of America

1 2 3 4 5 6 11 10 09 08 07 06

Library of Congress Cataloging-in-Publication Data
Rustad, Martha E. H. (Martha Elizabeth Hillman), 1975–
Today is hot / by Martha E.H. Rustad.
p. cm.—(Pebble plus. How's the weather?)
Summary: "Simple text and photographs present weather information, clothing choices, and activities for a hot day"—Provided by publisher.
Includes bibliographical references and index.
ISBN-13: 978-0-7368-5343-9 (hardcover)
ISBN-10: 0-7368-5343-X (hardcover)
1. Weather—Juvenile literature. 2. Hot weather clothing—Juvenile literature. 3. Active learning—Hot weather conditions—Juvenile literature. I. Title. II. Series.
QC981.3.R88 2006
551.5—dc22 2005020791

Editorial Credits
Sarah L. Schuette, editor; Ted Williams, designer; Jo Miller, photo researcher; Scott Thoms, photo editor

Photo Credits
BananaStock Ltd., 11, 15
Capstone Press/Karon Dubke, cover (child), 1, 9, 13, 19, 20–21
Corbis/Craig Tuttle, 21 (inset); Dex Images Inc., 17; LWA-Dann Tardif, 4–5; Richard Klune, cover (window)
SuperStock/age fotostock, 6–7

The author dedicates this book to her son, Leif Anton Rustad.

Note to Parents and Teachers

The How's the Weather? set supports national science standards related to climate and weather. This book describes and illustrates a hot day. The images support early readers in understanding the text. The repetition of words and phrases helps early readers learn new words. This book also introduces early readers to subject-specific vocabulary words, which are defined in the Glossary section. Early readers may need assistance to read some words and to use the Table of Contents, Glossary, Read More, Internet Sites, and Index sections of the book.

Table of Contents

A Hot Day 4
What I Wear 10
What We Do 14
How's the Weather? 20

Glossary 22
Read More 23
Internet Sites 23
Index 24

A Hot Day

The weather is hot today.

It is summertime.

The temperature is high
on a hot day.
The air outside is humid.

The sun shines down.
It feels warm and sticky.

What I Wear

I wear shorts and a T-shirt
on a hot day.
My clothes help me stay cool.

I wear a swimming suit
at the pool.
I put sunscreen
on my skin.

What We Do

We visit the beach
on a hot day.
We wiggle our toes
in the warm sand.

We play outside
in the heat.
We get sweaty
and thirsty.

We rest in the shade.
We drink water
to keep cool.

igloo

How's the Weather?

Today is hot.

What will the weather

be like tomorrow?

Glossary

air—the gasses around the earth; we need air to breathe.

humid—damp and moist

shade—an area that is out of the sun

summer—the season between spring and fall when the weather is warmest

temperature—the measure of how hot or cold something is

weather—the condition outdoors at a certain time and place; weather can be cold, hot, calm, windy, rainy, dry, sunny, or cloudy.

Read More

Chambers, Catherine. *Heat Wave.* Wild Weather. Chicago: Heinemann, 2002.

Thomas, Rick. *Sizzle!: A Book about Heat Waves.* Amazing Science. Minneapolis: Picture Window Books, 2005.

Walker, Sally M. *Heat.* Early Bird Energy. Minneapolis: Lerner, 2006.

Internet Sites

FactHound offers a safe, fun way to find Internet sites related to this book. All of the sites on FactHound have been researched by our staff.

Here's how:

1. Visit *www.facthound.com*
2. Type in this special code **073685343X** for age-appropriate sites. Or enter a search word related to this book for a more general search.
3. Click on the **Fetch It** button.

FactHound will fetch the best sites for you!

Index

air, 6
beach, 14
clothes, 10
humid, 6
outside, 6, 16
shade, 18
summertime, 4
sun, 8
sunscreen, 12
swimming suit, 12
temperature, 6
today, 4, 20
tomorrow, 20
warm, 8, 14
water, 18
weather, 4, 20

Word Count: 108
Grade: 1
Early-Intervention Level: 13